Thoughts and Metaphors

A N E

Dedication:
This is for the lost ones, the wandering souls, for those who
feel they don't belong, the ones on the outside looking in. I
hope reading this will remind you that you are not alone &
that someone cares about you. I care about you. Even if this
book isn't your cup of tea, I truly wish you the best & hope
you find a place where you feel you belong. Please, just don't
give up.

Thoughts & Metaphors: A Journal of Poems by A N E
Second Edition
ISBN: 979-8-9879115-0-1

Table of Contents

The Darkness That Surrounds Me

Alone: A Nightmare
It's the moment,
I was told,
that is heart-shattering;
When you're hit with so much shock
that the pounding in your chest &
all the physical pain
are only a small afterthought.
That moment when you realize
you're alone after all,
completely & forever.
This is a moment
I've heard so much about
but it's nothing like what they said,
the feeling doesn't shatter my heart
it walks into my life
as if it were an old friend.

Dark Place

There's a dark place
that my mind falls into sometimes,
taking my heart with it.
It steals all feeling
leaving a numbing void inside,
locking away my motivation
somewhere I cannot find.
These days become harder to live &
nights never seem long enough;
Tasks as simple as
forcing myself out of bed
feels like lifting the weight
of a thousand men,
while paralyzed completely.
Every word has the power
to pull me deeper,
though few have the power
to bring me out again.
It's not something I willingly choose
but an illness that has chosen me.
It doesn't define who I am
or where I'm going,
just a battle I fight daily
where I value my victories &
press past my losses.

Something More
I wish I could do better
in this life.
I wish
to accomplish more,
to fail less,
to do things
that are meaningful to me.
To be someone
that people are proud of,
not the failure,
the disappointment
they're embarrassed by &
are trying to hide.
Maybe one day I'll be more
than I am,
I just know
that I'm discontent
standing here
so still.

Anxiety Attack
This world is closing in &
I'm finding it hard
to catch my breath.
This place is too small,
my heart feels claustrophobic,
my head is spinning, &
my palms are sweaty.
If only I knew
where to go from here
or how to get back
to the way things
once were.

Lonely

Loneliness, for me,
does not come from being alone.
Loneliness is sitting in a crowded room.
Loneliness is going unnoticed
by ones you love most.
Loneliness is being torn down & hurt
by those you thought you could trust,
without anyone willing to defend you.
Loneliness is company without connection.
Lonely is what I feel
when I'm emotionally drained
around people who need me.
To be alone is one thing,
to feel lonely is entirely different.

The Scars That Never Heal
Sticks & stones lay in a pile
on the floor.
Though they may bruise me &
make me bleed,
they'll never scar
quite like the words
you left on my skin.
Those words you used
against me
time & time again,
ones that hurt me
in ways I'll never
truly heal from.

Deep Cuts

You used your words against me,
like a knife
cutting deep into my soul.
You kept saying you loved me,
as if it were an excuse
to beat me down.
I felt it was all my fault,
if I did better
then maybe you'd treat me
like I was worth something,
anything at all.
I felt so guilty
wanting to leave,
as you played the victim.
I wish I had known,
it was all an act.
Now that you're gone,
I carry the weight
of this hurt you left behind
on my own.

I Still Care
The heaviness,
it wears me down &
I worry
my heart
can't handle it.
The pain keeps piling up,
my soul is reaching its limits;
How much more can I take
before I stop letting people in?
Before my heart
forgets how to love?
I'm done blaming myself,
I'm done defending you,
saying I must've done something
to justify the way you treated me.
You made a choice,
now I make mine;
Though all the pain
you put me through,
I choose not to hurt you back.
You shattered my heart
but, I hope,
that you never have to find out
what that feels like.
Though you destroyed our friendship,
I still care;
Though I no longer trust you,
I forgive you.

Broken Heart

In my chest
beats the shattered pieces
of a broken heart.
Once it had been whole &
full of hope,
it beat strong & hard
for the idea of love.
Ripped out & thrown to the ground,
stomped on,
walked over,
broken, &
frail;
There wasn't much left
of this heart of mine.
In my pain,
I gathered up the broken parts
locking them in
a heart-shaped box,
pretending to be whole again;
Hoping no one sees
what you did to me.
It still beats in my chest,
this broken heart,
begging to never be hurt
that way again.

My Anxious Mind
I often get this sinking feeling
that I've ruined it all this time &
lost my chance
at knowing your heart.
Spending hours
longing to go back
to a point where I could fix this,
to prepare myself better,
to do the right thing
this time around,
to have a second chance
at being your friend;
Understanding you better,
loving you for who you are &
earning your love in return.
Some nights
I question what it'd be like
sharing this adventure
called life
with you.

Autumn Leaf: A Metaphor
I am an autumn leaf,
swishing & swaying
in the wind.
I once was a part of a whole,
living somewhere
I felt I belonged;
Now I am nothing,
belonging nowhere,
only floating through life.
I use to push against the wind,
discontent with where I was at,
now I am learning to fly.
I see that I had been caged before,
now I am free.

I am an autumn leaf &
my time grows short
as I hit the ground,
waiting to wither away.

Shadows: A Nightmare

This dark shadow is cast over my soul,
they follow my steps
whether by day or by night.
A curse I cannot rid myself of,
these nightmares find me
no matter where I go
or where I hide.
If only they'd stay in my sleep,
giving me peace & sanctuary in daylight;
Yet, here they are,
slowly down a hallway they'll come &
I don't know why they're here.
They can scare me all they want
but jokes on them,
because I do not fear death
so they have no real power over me.
When my time comes,
I'll look death in the face
with peace in my heart &
smile.

Screams: A Nightmare
Walking down a lonely hallway
I can hear her screams;
I know in my mind that she isn't real,
still, the sound of a banshee's cry
rings in my ears.
She's there around the next corner
her hands, like black spider webs,
stick to either side of the wall
blocking my path.
She is made up entirely of scribbles
from all the papers I've ever thrown away;
She collects these small failures,
they make her stronger.
Though she has no face
I feel her staring back at me,
looking straight into my soul.
She tries to pull towards me
but she cannot move
for her webbed hands chain her to the wall;
She lets out another cry
revealing her mouth, too, was webbed shut.
This cry was different than the last,
she cries out in pain & longing,
trying to draw my soul to hers
but I'm too scared.
I'm afraid to admit these failures &
I know I'm not strong enough
to stand up to her.
As I walk away,
she cries out again in rage &
I let her screams haunt me.

Depression: A Nightmare
I sit across from her,
face to face with a mirrored image of myself.
Her hair is orange, like fire,
opposed to my golden blonde,
it glows wet from the sweat
building on her head.
I'm confused by what I'm seeing
or why I'm even here;
When my hand moves, hers does too,
I knew it was me on the other side.
Sweat continues to build on my reflection,
before long, her face starts melting away &
she begins to scream;
Her gestures still faintly mirror mine,
yet, I am not hurt.
She forced her eyes to lift & meet mine
as they start to burn away too, &
the image of her is burned to my mind.
Tears stream down my face
as she continues to melt away,
until every recognizable part of her
was completely gone.

A Light In
The Dark

Hope: A Metaphor
My world is dark.
The walls of life are closing in &
I'm suffocating here,
trapped in this place
I don't belong.
I'm tired of waking up
to everyday battles
I will never win,
thoughts of giving up
filling my mind.
Though, as I grow weary,
losing the strength to keep going on,
I see hope
fading in & out
like the light of a firefly.
It's enough
to help me carry on.

Okay

With damaged feelings &
this shattered heart
I now know
that sometimes
it's okay to not be okay.
Things will look up
just give it some time &,
for now,
just be.
You will keep moving forward,
you will keep growing,
this isn't the end for you.
So please,
don't stop existing.

Hating Myself
When I say I hate myself
it isn't what I really mean;
I mean the hundreds of phrases
that I've hidden inside my mind.
I hate my body,
I hate who I use to be,
I hate all these memories
that keep haunting me;
I hate it when I sleep in,
I hate that I feel
like I'm not enough,
I hate being so needy
by simply existing.
I hate feeling misunderstood,
I hate being viewed
as something I'm not;
I hate having to be a picky eater &
the comments that come along with it,
Or being seen as a burden
on those around me.
I hate all these little things about me &
so much more,
but I can look in the mirror &
see someone
who is trying her best.
I don't hate her.

Toxic
I find it hard
to put into words
what you do to me,
tearing me down
so you can feel better
about yourself.
You say you care about me,
but all your other words & actions
say the opposite.
When I try to talk
you tell me how hard
things have been,
as if to justify
your behavior.
Though I don't believe your excuses, &
I will not justify you,
I will stick around anyways;
Because I do care about you,
not about what you do for me.
If not me,
who will stay
to watch you grow
into the amazing person
you are meant to be.

Lamppost: A Metaphor
At the bottom of the lamppost
I buried my heart,
in hopes the light would one day
help me find it again.
Up from the ground
grew a vine of thorns & roses,
for my beauty was dangerous &
could easily heart;
But my love was soft yet strong,
like the frail rose,
in confidence,
Towering over the ground.
Maybe there in the ground
my heart would be safe,
maybe one day it'll be free,
or maybe when I die
then they'll see:
here at this lamppost
was buried a part of me.

Blue-Jay: A Metaphor

My heart is a blue-jay
trapped in this cage
we call depression.
It flutters around in circles
desperate for a way out,
barely seeing past
the metal bars it's stuck behind.
Oh, to see the sun again,
to soar with the wind
in my feathers.
Maybe someday.

Rainy Days
Rainy days are a comfort
for my anxious soul.
It is peace,
melting away fear
one drop at a time.
I find a sense of purity
in the petrichor &
solitude in the midst of the storms.

Saved

She has a heart so big,
so full of care
for those in her world
with such passion &
conviction,
she spent her whole life
saving those around her,
touching every soul.
Little does she know
that she needs to let people in,
so they can save her too.

Stars
Do you ever just look up
at the night sky &
are completely captivated
by the stars?
Drawn to them
as if they were calling out to you,
making you feel small
yet not forgotten;
they seem to whisper lightly
telling me that I am not alone &,
for once,
I almost believed it.

Priceless
The human soul
is like a priceless work of art
on display for the world to see.
Some are confused by your complexity,
some don't like the way
you are painted;
Some don't understand your purpose &
some will try to make you
feel like a mistake.
Don't lose hope,
for others will see your deep beauty &
appreciate the perfectly imperfect design
given to you.
Listen to those who understand you &
don't let the world
make you believe
you're valued as anything less
than priceless.

Winter

The snowy landscapes sparkle
under the light of the rising sun,
the brown tree branches
become heavy with snow so pure
it seemed to shine.
The scene was framed
by the icicles hanging from my window
while a red cardinal sings its song
from the feeder just outside.
The beauty of winter
is breathtaking for a heart
willing to appreciate
what they see.

Promise

Every morning
there is a sunrise,
it is a promise for today.
A promise for a chance
at a fresh start,
you just have to take it;
A promise for kinder words,
if only you are willing
to speak them to yourself;
A promise for a happier life,
if you look at what you have
instead of what you don't &
choose to be grateful;
A promise for love,
if you will show love to others
as you learn to love yourself too.
Today is a promise
because tomorrow isn't guaranteed.

All The Thoughts
Inside My Head

Metaphors
Her mind was beautiful
though few would see
the fascinating world
inside her head;
So full of stories & metaphors
for even the smallest
  things,
        words, &
              phrases in life.
Pictures painted inside her mind,
galaxies surround her imagination.
Slow in speech &
so lost in thoughts,
how hard it must be
to go through every day
translating words
into a language
this world would understand.
What a beautiful curse to have.

Silence
Silence says to me
what you will not.
I can read your feelings
like a book opened to
just the right page,
telling me more than
your words could express.
Silence is only uncomfortable
for those who cannot
hear it speak.

Untitled I
Focus,
        lacking.
Thoughts constantly trailing off.
Was it here?
Or maybe over there?
What had I been looking for, again?
Mind!
Ah, yes, peace of mind.
  Slowly
          it
            is
              drifting
                    away.

Known

I wish I could tell you
all the things
I hold in my heart;
All the good,
all the bad, &
some things that fit in between.
To know
that someone knows me wholly &
still wants me
for who I am.

Loud Minds

Some say I'm loud
when I chose to speak
yet, I don't notice;
For the sound is nothing
in comparison
to the noise inside my head.

My mind is always running,
overwhelmed by the world around me,
trying to process everything in it.
How I long for a moment of silence
away from the world &
void of my own thoughts.
How wonderful it would be
to just exist for a while.

Red Balloon: A Metaphor
My anxiety
is a big red balloon
floating away &
when it gets too high,
I need someone
to come & anchor me
back down to the ground.

Crazy
Sometimes I wonder
if talking to yourself
is really all that crazy
when no one else
will listen.
I write to myself &
that's honestly
the same thing for me.

Quietly

Quietly I follow along
listening to the words spoken &
Enjoying time spent together.
You scold me for not talking much &
ask me why I'm always so upset,
as if my silence was something wrong
or something to be punished for.
"Please try to understand me better,"
I plea silently,
Hoping you'll realize
that this is who I am &
I don't need to make loud noise
to enjoy your company.
I'm not ignoring you,
nor am I upset;
I am listening,
caught on every word,
trying to understand you better.
My silence isn't a flaw.
Listening sincerely,
I'm just being me
trying to show you I care,
We all show care
in different ways.

The Mask

Every day I put on this mask
hiding from the world around me.
I become what others need,
helping them however I can;
My needs don't matter as much
I'll figure out how to meet them
on my own,
hiding my struggles
from those around me.
The mask hides them well,
I dare not take it off
out of fear of becoming a burden
or something to pity.
When wearing the mask
I hope I'm seen as strong.
No one can see the tears
welling up on the other side,
no one ever will, &
when I'm all alone
where I know it's safe,
I'll take the mask off &
let it all out.

Flawed
Something needs to change
though I'm not sure what.
I am flawed
in ways that I'm not sure
I'll ever know how to fix.

Untitled II
My mind is a chaotic place &
I, like you,
am confused by its complexity.
I write
to sort out my thoughts & feelings
in the hope
that it'll help me learn
to better understand myself &
figure out who I am.

Misunderstood
She often wondered
why she felt so alone
in a world so full of people.
Her thoughts felt so distant
from those around her;
She could see their hearts &
she understood their souls,
yet, she knew
that no one will ever be able
to do the same for her.

Disappear
The world around me
is so loud,
so overwhelming,
sometimes my soul can't take it.
I wish I could take a break,
to be away from everything
for a little bit longer.
How I long
for a moment of silence,
a moment of peace
in this noisy world.
Would it be okay
if I simply disappeared
only for a little while.

Falling Behind
Sometimes
I feel as though
in this world
I'm falling behind
because I keep stopping
to take in the scenery
as I go
instead of rushing
to my destination.

Untitled III
Your words
cause sparks inside my heart
making me smile.
All the things
you're letting me learn
about you,
it's a privilege
that I don't get
very often
anymore.

Untitled IV
She's a quiet girl,
reserved in nature,
but a soul like a lion
roaring inside of her.

The Ways of The Wind

How beautiful are the songs it sings
understood by few
in this world around us.
Do you hear its songs?
Do you understand its stories?
These stories that man cannot tell,
they are whispered by the wind
if only you'll listen.
Stories of days past,
of battles won,
of those we've lost,
of things to come.
You say that the wind is silent
but you've never truly tried to hear it.
Stop.
Breathe in.
Breathe out.
Calm your heart &
just listen.
The ways of the wind are only for those
who are willing to understand.

Freedom Calling Me

Freedom: A Metaphor

At the edge of the forest
I hear freedom calling me,
howling like a wolf in the night.
She calls me into the woods
drawn to her
as if she were a part of me,
something I had lost &
need to find again.
She showed me the world
through her eyes,
she had truly been free
having the right to be anywhere
So long as she chose to go.
It caught my heart,
like a bird ready to flutter away,
to see her loyalty lay here
outshining all else.
The pack she had
she was with to the end.
She chose to stay,
to protect the weak,
to help the strong.
Freedom wasn't a lone wolf
like I had always pictured;
She didn't run,
but stood her ground.
She was fighting for her purpose
with a passion,
choosing integrity & trust
over power.

Growth

I've changed so much
in these last few days,
weeks,
months,
shutting the door
on who I once was.
Learning to love
without condition,
to help
without being asked,
to listen
without judgment.
I still have a long way to go &
I'm no where near perfect
but I won't stop trying
until I'm finished
making up for
everything I've done
in my past.

A Blessing In Disguise

I never thought
there would come a day
where I'd have to learn
how to live without you.
I cried so hard,
I felt so dead,
how could you hurt me like this?
I was bitter
for so long
but now I want to say
thank you;
For when you left
I found myself again
in the pile of broken pieces.
I figured out how to live again,
learning to love more
than I have before &
becoming confident
in who I decided to be.

Worth
Here in this life
I'm starting to find my worth.
It does not lay in opinions
of those around me,
whether they be friend or foe,
for who are they
to determine my value?

It is not found
in the man who doesn't want me &
says I won't find love,
for respecting myself & my body
enough to say no.

It is not found
written on a price tag
hanging on my arm
like a sweater at the mall.

My worth is found
as I learn to love
who I really am;
Knowing the truest version of myself
found only in the One
who created my soul.
Where the world sees
an unlovable soul,
God sees
someone worth dying for.

Destinations
It's hard for me to understand
where life is taking me anymore.
so many bumps & bruises
along this way,
I often wonder
if I'm even heading the right direction.
My heart is telling me
that there has to be another way,
one that is safer for me;
Yet, I trust the one
who is navigating my journey,
for I know
It'll be okay
even when I don't know
my destination.

Apologies
The hardest apology to accept
is always the one
you never received
but the only way to heal,
to move on,
is to forgive them
even if they aren't sorry.
Love them still,
even if they don't deserve it
because you're better than this,
than to stoop to their level.
They are only human,
we all make mistakes, &
everyone is in need of a little love
so be the one to show it anyways.

Time

Time is an existing potential,
relative only
to the person living in it.
One person's long day
can be another person's
blinking moment.
Some think life takes forever
to catch up with them,
While others saw it
as a passing memory.
No matter how time
appears to you
remember to
spend it wisely.

Introvert
People underestimate
the power of solitude &
the energy found
in spending time alone.

Scars
The scars we wear
do not map out
future destinations,
they only tell stories
of our past
showing the world
how strong we are.

To Be In The Sun
Sand beneath my feet,
the touch of sun
against my pale skin,
there is something
so therapeutic
about laying beside the water &
letting your mind
just
wander off.

Lead Foot
I often think
of how humbling it would be
to meet the man
that nearly ended my life;
To look him in the eyes &
know that he held
the fate of my world
in his hands
for a moment of time.
To recognize his existence
putting a face
with this idea of him
I have inside my head.
Seeing the reality of him
as a soul,
to know that he has
a life of his own;
to see him as a father
rather than a lead foot.
To see his heart
past the dodge truck
would give me a sense of closure.
I hope, one day, to shake his hand &
thank him
for changing my life
in ways I can't explain
or ever return from.

Change

It's in the middle
of all this that I finally realized
how important it is
to forgive myself too;
Letting go of past regrets &
moving on from
who I once was,
as I find
who I'm meant to be.

Music
Every note she played
had sparked a color,
filling the air around her.
Who she played for
no longer mattered
for she was lost
in the beauty of the art
she created inside her mind.
Music meant more to her
than hitting the right notes &
following sheet music;
It was passion &
the ability to play
in such a way
that you find yourself in the sound,
showing the world your soul
one song at a time.
Music is simply
painting a picture
in the air,
using sound as your color &
passion as your brush.

The Door Slam

Selfless Destruction
I use to brag on my selflessness,
using the neglect of my own wellbeing
as if it were proof
of this statement.
Self-abuse doesn't equal selflessness,
I was just too blind to see
the casualties I left in my path.
I walked around destroying lives,
throwing away relationships,
only helping those who cry out in pain
while hurting myself the least.
I didn't think twice
about ruining someone else's life
because I could look back &
see the few I saved
mixed with the damage I caused myself.
Self care opens your eyes
to see the world around you more clearly
&
those souls you destroyed so long ago,
making you never want to go back
to the way things were.

Self Care
How hard it is
to start again,
to take care of your own soul
for the first time in a while.
It's always the hardest
to take that first step,
it's like you're meeting yourself
for the first time.
Just be patient,
like every new friend
you have to take the time
getting to know yourself.
When you've neglected
your soul so long,
you'll find
that even your smallest likes &
interests
could have changed.
So, sit down,
a cup of coffee in hand &
spend time with yourself,
figuring out who you are &
falling in love
with the person
you are meant to be.

Michigan: A Metaphor
She was cold to touch
but warm at heart,
full of love & laughter
behind a sad smile.
Depression sinking in
no one would see
sharp edges,
deep cuts,
Michigan never left my side.
She saw my soul,
she knew my heart,
she kept my secrets.
A run down piano keys,
I'm lost in a song,
note by note
the world would know me
if only they tried.
Laying under maple trees
there were story tellings &
deep contemplations,
she carried her load &
half mine too;
Things were easier
with Michigan around.
These days grow colder,
night is coming,
a splash of color in a dimly lit sky.
Darkness fell,
heaving a sigh, &
my days with Michigan were gone.

Words

Words are a powerful magic.
They can build people up &
they can tear them down
just as easily.
You hold this power
in the very palm of your hand.
Think wisely before you use it,
for even the absence of words
speaks volumes.

What I'm Not
The reflection I see in the mirror
is my greatest curse,
the most deceptive part
of who I am.
I've been told I'm too thin,
that I should stop starving myself;
I've been told that "real" men
only want women with the right curves.
To be torn down &
made fun of
for something out of my control,
you treat me like it's wrong
to have insecurities about my weight
when you're the one who gave me insecurities
in the first place.
No one should have to feel this way,
no matter their size,
because it doesn't determine
who they are on the inside.
My body is the biggest distraction I have
from who I really am.

Finally Myself
I often talked a lot growing up
because I was raised
to be polite
but talking makes me nervous.
I would ramble on & on,
talking far too much, &
feeling less myself
with every sentence.
It built up a reputation &
now I can't be quiet
without someone thinking
it has to mean something:
I'm upset
or mad at someone;
Maybe I'm sad
or scared;
but they never stopped to think
that maybe I'm just finally
being myself.

Learning

I think part of growing up
is realizing that
life doesn't always turn out
just like you imagined it would.
We are never as alone
as we think we are,
we just need to keep growing
until we learn how to see that.

Attention
For the first time
in the while,
I seem to have caught
someone's eye.
All they see of me
is what I don't know,
the things they don't like,
what I can't do, &
all I cannot be.
This isn't what I wanted,
please let me
fade into the background
once more.

Heavy

My heart is heavy
for the world around me,
such pain,
such grief,
overwhelming my soul.
I hear your heart,
I caught your feeling,
such strong emotion
you're carrying on your own.
How I long to fix it,
to take away your hurt,
to make you happy again,
to see you smile.
This is my prayer,
my plea,
my cry,
for the pain to stop &
the world to know
how to love again.

The Door-Slam

Be careful how you treat
the girl who loves
with a full heart,
for she's been through hell &
back again.
She's a light
in this darkened world,
choosing only to see the good
in people around her,
ignoring the bad.
She can handle so much,
letting your words
cut into her soul &
your actions
create a heaviness in her heart,
giving you the power to break her.
she'll forgive your wrongs
time & time again
but beware,
for when she finally shatters,
she will be cold as ice,
feeling nothing at all.
The girl who once felt so much,
so deeply,
will become calm
as she finally figures out
how to walk away.
Once she's gone,
she's never coming back.

The Letters You'll Never Read
In an old notebook
I pour my heart out on the pages,
saying all the words
I can't say to your face.
I've talked about wolves &
the way the stars seem to shine;
I tell you about my day &
my music obsessions;
I rant my latest theories &
the importance
of the color blue.
I've shown my feelings,
I left some pages tear stained, &
these are what make up
the letters you'll never read.

Walls

I build up these walls to my heart
just to see them torn down.
I trust no one &
everyone
at the same time.
I crave deep connections
but fear being hurt
by those same people,
so I shut them out
before they can get too close.
I'm torn between wanting company &
wishing I could just be alone.
I don't understand myself enough
to know how to make this work,
I just wish life was easier than this.

Doors
I am a series of open doors
to those I feel
may accept me for who I am.
Though cautious at first,
when I trust,
it's always to the fullest extent;
If you destroy that trust
or prove me wrong,
the next door
will leave you with
nothing more than a brick wall.

Coming Home

Home
If home is where the heart is
then I have yet to settle down.
My heart is still wandering,
searching for a place to rest
where it is full of love &
my soul is completely accepted.
I am longing a place of peace,
with moments of joy & laughter
shared with those I love.
My soul is still looking
for the place where it belongs &
once I find it
I'll finally feel like I'm coming home.

Instrumental Stories
All music holds power
in the stories that are told
with every song heard.
Instrumental music
is a special kind of magic
because it doesn't tell it's own story,
it tells you the one
that's locked away
inside your imagination.
No two people will ever find
the same story inside a song,
for each story you find
will be your own.

Books
Nothing heals my heart
or recharges my soul
quite like running away from reality
to an unknown world.
To be caught up in someone else's story,
standing in their shoes,
feeling their emotions
until they become as real
as you or me.
It shows me I am not alone &
reminds me
to look beyond myself.

Love
It's more than just a word.
It's more than the short phrase
that escapes your lips so often.
It's all about what you do
to show them you care so much.
Words that don't act,
they are dead
for when you love someone
it becomes more than just
an empty word.
Instead,
it becomes so many tiny things,
small actions,
little touches,
encouraging phrases,
thoughtful gifts,
moments of time;
Listening to them &
finding new ways
to say "I love you,"
you learn the language
their soul speaks in.
Hoping they'll start to see themselves
the way you see them.

Friends

Here's to the unexpected friends.
The ones you didn't plan to meet
whom your soul felt drawn to
the moment you said
your first hello.

Here's to the understanding friends.
The ones with whom
you can share your heart &
be your complete self,
knowing they'll accept you for who you are.

Here's to the honest friends.
The ones bluntly telling you
what you need to hear
rather than blindly supporting you
into your horrible mistakes.
The ones who see the big picture &
love you enough
to shove you in the right direction.

Here's to the comfortable friends.
The ones you love to hang out with &
jump to see
because being around them
feels like coming home.

Perspective
It's a beautiful thing
to see yourself
in someone else's eyes,
to catch even a glimpse
of what they see in you.
Maybe then you'll see
past all of your flaws &
realize how wonderful
you really are.
To observe your strength,
to know your importance, &
to see how much you mean to me.

Where I Belong
In a world
where I felt unlovable &
misunderstood,
God gave me you
to show me I was wrong.
Every day I know you,
you show me I'm loved;
Every word spoken
reminds me that
there is a place
where I belong.

Untitled V
Looking back
I found that
on the days
where I felt
my world was crashing down
around me,
it was really just God,
putting everything into place.

Distance
There is a comfort
in looking up
at this night sky we share.
You may not be here with me
but we both look up
at the same stars,
so maybe we aren't
as far away
as we think we are.

The End of Me

Here we are,
yet again,
at the end of me.
I am brought to the edge
of who I've been
every time my heart grabs a hold
of those precious words,
it's as if they were written
just for me.
In that moment,
as tears stream down my face,
I realize that
even when the world said
I wasn't worth it,
that I'm not worth being loved
you were there, Lord, &
you loved me for everything I was.
Even when friends stopped talking to me,
making me feel so alone
in this present world,
you were there,
reminding me that I am not alone.
You are always here
when I need you most,
showing me
nothing can separate me from your love.

The Stories We Write
We write
because there is a story
our souls long to read,
it just doesn't exist
yet.

Poem Title: She Will- Written by a Friend
"For You, going forward :)"

She is oblivious, I think.
Oblivious to her light
for it shines brighter than she could ever know.
Her brilliance,
for it inspires and awakens.
Her beauty,
for she is breathtaking in a way heretofore unknown.
Her depth,
for she is an ocean in a world of streams.
She is oblivious to these things not due to naivete
or youth
or inexperience
but, rather, in a beautiful twist of irony
oblivious due to those very aforementioned
qualities themselves.
Qualities which she possesses in radiant abundance
she is a kaleidoscope of wonder,
a glorious human being in every way.
A rare flower that blooms when others fade,
a flower that shines bright when skies are grey,
a lily in a field of roses.
She is every sunrise and every sunset.
She knows not, the strength in which she possesses
the difference she makes to those in her life,
the happiness that is due to her presence in this world.
I believe in her,
with a certainty that cannot even begin to be described.
Though from afar it may be
one need not be near to see her light,
to feel her magic,
to witness her splendor,
to be touched by her soul.
The stars shine for her,
the rain dances upon the earth for her,
the sun rises each morning to see her.
Her future may be unwritten

89

but the pages will be filled with beauty,
with happiness,
with contentment.
She knows it not at this moment
but she will…

Note From The Author

I hope you enjoy reading the revised 2nd edition of my poetry compilation. I tried to keep the changes minimum and mostly technical. Though some of the words I had written in 2017 make me cringe, this is my first book and I'm so proud of the girl I was back then. She went through hell and came out stronger for it.

She moved halfway across the country on a whim and went on every adventure she could until she figured out who she was. Without her, I wouldn't be who I am today.

So this is your reminder that no matter how much your past self makes you cringe, just remember that if they hadn't gone through what they did or made the mistakes they had, you wouldn't be here today. It's a scary though. You don't have to like your past self to thank them for who you are today.

Much love,

Anastasia

A N E

Follow Me:
@a_n_e_poetry (Instagram)
@nepenthepoetry (Facebook)
@anewritingservices (TikTok)

Acknowledgements (Unedited, 2017):

Molly- Thank you for being the one who bought me my first poetry book & pushed me to write a book after you saw the poetry scribbled in my notebook. You are the kind of friend that is strong enough to lean on. You stand up for me when I can't & you are always willing to bluntly tell me how it is. I'm lucky to have ever met you.

Haley- Thank you for being the one that helped me become the writer I am today. You are the friend that calms me down when I'm being too emotional and you remind me that there is always a better way. You are always so gentle but firm when you need to be. You comfort me when I'm crying and help me back on my feet. I don't know where my life would be without you.

Tom- Well bud, you've tolerated me this long and you've proofread many a poem for me. Thank you for sticking with me, I couldn't have gotten through so many long days without you. I'm sure by now you're starting to go crazy because of me, but I appreciate you always being light-hearted and lifting every mood.

Rick-thank you for always questioning everything, pushing me to be the best that I can be. You've always been the kind of support I need and you are always there on those darker days to show me where the light is.

To the friend who wished to remain unnamed- You know who you are. I value your friendship very much and I hope to know you for the rest of our lives, even if we don't talk every day. You are a remarkable human being and the world is lucky to have you in it.

Acknowledgements (2023)

Dakota- My love, you are the reason I write. My biggest cheerleader and closest friend. I don't know what I'd do without you. You love me at my worst and you celebrate me at my best. You make life a little more worth while.

Brenda- I know you're reading this, scoffing at the idea of not being listed as my first acknowledgement. Just know that I love you all the same. You found me at some of my lowest times and darkest hours but my darkness never scared you. My constant inspiration.

www.ingramcontent.com/pod-product-compliance
Lightning Source LLC
Chambersburg PA
CBHW060337130626
46553CB00003B/1037